JUST SUPPOSE

Maura Johnston

I

Published in 1999 by
Lonnra Press,
Muff,
Co. Donegal
Ireland

A CIP record for this book is available from the British Library.

ISBN 0-9531707-1-3

Cover Illustration by Helen Johnston

Printed by Colour Books, Dublin

Photograph by Leon McAuley

II

Acknowledgements

Acknowledgements are made to the editors of the following publications in which some of these poems appeared:
Ulster Tatler, (December 1984), *The Belfast Review* (Spring 1985), *Poetry Ireland* (Autumn 1985), *The Female Line* (November 1986), *Poetry Ireland* (Autumn 1986), *Orbis Quarterly, Sunday Tribune, Fingerpost* (Second Prize), *Honest Ulsterman, H.U.* (1994), *Cookstown Jottings* (1994), *Fingerpost* (September 1994), *The Linnet* (Spring 1995), *The Linnet* (Spring 1996), *Thoughts into Words* (1997), *Moving On* (1998), *H.U.* (Autumn 1998).

I would like to thank Sive Haughey for her encouragement and support in publishing this collection.

I would also like to thank Cookstown Council for the bursary awarded to the Tyrone Guthrie Centre, Annamakerrig.

For
Kevin

FATHER FIGURE

The lost-soul moan of wind in the wires
And benweed poking patterns in the grass
Like jaundiced fingers of doom
Sift through my shifting memories
That settle in a mottled morass
And twist new shapes in this room.

I almost feel the brittle crust
Of cold that made the hurricane
Clam in my hand, and
Slid his shadow monstrous
On the meal house wall, pinned
There prosperous, the self-made man.

We saw an owl once, in the front field,
Sagged in a secret of feathers, waiting.
That was in the twilight when
He fingered grasses to gauge a yield,
Or lovingly leaned on a gate,
His acres before him.

We worked the hay for him, trying to make
The music he could with a worn
Wooden rake along a green swathe.
Our notes wavered, got weak.
We are scattered. Alone
I can face him now, unafraid.

ONE AUTUMN

A frog came into the kitchen
Right in the middle of the fourth

Decade, the one I gave out.
It sat where the tilley poured

Its humming yellow circle. We
Wouldn't touch it in case of warts

And anyway the prayers continued
In drones and cushion muffle snorts

Of laughter, to the last of the trimmings.
Then we tried to catch it

On a shoe box lid, to tip it
Back awkward into the sated

Settled Autumn night.
Hectored, its blotched horny

Hide could barely bind its
Tiny pulse of life. Cornered

It sprang, with a sudden
Retching rise, right into

2

A basin of apple jelly. All
Day it had dripped, thin

Amber drops, essence of stubble
Fields and tightening dusk.

Crab apples. Gnarled old trees,
Arthritic contours masking

Plenty, like a barren bitch
Suckling twins. The flour bag

Swung, slung between table
And window, its sour

Squeezings ransoming her
Hours of hobbled hooking. Next

Day she gave it to the pigs,
Reluctantly, sad to let

Go her share in one
More Autumn.

THE LOUP SCHOLARS
(for the O'Briens of Mowillian)

Distance pulls like spun sugar
The brittle threads of sound
That waver, rise, echo in
The bowl of afternoon.

A whoop, a shove and a shout
The Loup scholars are out,
Out through the gate, bucketing
Like wee calves loosed in spring.

Time saunters alongside them
Halting at every hole
In the hedge, offering
Sweet sorrel, bitter berries.

James, John and Anna run, run,
Run past the trailing rest,
Boots thumping, elbows pumping,
Breath failing in their breasts,

Slitting the skin of summer
To expose the yellowed
Underlay that cushions
Thinly the coming cold.

MOTHER

Palms upward on her apron
Her hands were vulnerable as
An upturned beetle. Her fingers
Jerked, and her eyes were closed.
Her eyelids, fragile as a fly wing
Fluttering translucent, covered my childhood world.
I saw her on her high framed bike
Proud as Maeve, rigid as her conscience,
Respectably steering through the flat guild town.
We gathered sticks in the planting;
Sweetly crumbling ones, bark to light the fire.
She broke the long ones with a practised stamp,
And we heaped them on an old potato bag,
One he had finished with.
Carrying the knobbly bundle home I
Staggered at one end. She held the other in a
Knotted hand, and pushed a path for us.
She sang as she churned, the thin voice
Finely catching in the rhythm of the beaters,
Splashing my mind with sentiment
As the pungent buttermilk slapped the sides.
My daughter has the same small voice
That huddles over sleeping dolls
As my mother's songs once garnered dreams for me.

BABES IN THE WOOD

Birds, like notes of music on the wires;
Hearts ease water grey among the trees.
dreams of death plucked mutely on a lyre
And wisps of cradled ecstasies.
Their shoulders gleamed so whitely, lightly.
Slender bones, and glistening fronds of hair.
Leaves honeycombed the curve of knee
And neck nape.
Sleep sodden lids, heavy, heavy. There
The witch thorn prickle clawed so near them
A nose-twitch off, a jagged scrap of fur.
No swollen berry hung, a tender token
Weed smoke sagged in the matted air.

FRUSTRATION

Caressing the wind with fingertips.
Ignoring the roar.
Consciously loving the wail and sob
And scream of masochistic joy
Wrung from the wild, wet, weeping treetops.
Bend then, twist.
You cannot move to offer anything.
You love the stinging wet that trembles on
you.
Refuse all joy, joy filled.
Bend then, twist.
Grow and green and all the world
Won't mind your seeming selfish love.
I'll kiss the wind and help the rain
With clearer drops of mine.

AT NIGHT

I love the night sky,
Its cobweb coursing clouds dark
And light against deep dark
Flirting with a mellow careless moon.

In the night I fear
Nothing that moves,
Nothing that lives or loves,
But I have fears.
My own end cankers all,
A devil worm of desperation
That slyly feeds on me
And spawns carious comfort
In that I am.

There are other comforts.
Cradled in love it is easy to forget, until all
Splits, and feathered tentacles
Of thought freeze the face
A million miles close,
Close above mine.
And the moon leers down.

WAYS OF DYING

The street, that evening in June,
Gasping in the gasworks' quilted
Hum, had girls to fling round
Lamposts, timing their little
Cries to mine. I rose to your
Coming, eager, unused, in a
Room flaked with summer.
I've always wanted, since then,
A house facing West. Here
The days go unnoticed, slip
From us, familiar beads
Rattling our loosening grip.

I LOVED YOU

I loved you when the tears of laburnum
Blotted out the drabness of the streets.
We laughed together in the shadow of the
dungeons
By the waves that ribbed
The blackened, moth-holed rocks.
We feared little then.
Our lives seemed bound together
For the whole round gladness of our days.
We bathed ourselves in life, in every pool
That cupped the image of our golden dreams.
Now we are bound indeed. Our gilded city
Has grown bars of stone
That cage us in to fret against
The bonds we plaited.
Petal hard they cling, and tenderly
Confine us, stranded dreamless, starless.

AUTUMN

Autumn.
Your seaweed strands of hair fanned out
Upon my pillow
The light gold hazed, mist-webbed,
Gleamed dim
Within the cottage that crouched over us,
Fat hen
Feathering us. Indrawing time enriching
The lethargy of every lovely move.
Slow as the fall of
One uncertain leaf
Turning
Burning.

ULSTER 1972

I

I came from fields flat and green
Where cows knee deep stood stolid
With twitching ears and flicking tails.
I passed my boyhood there
Walking behind them in the evenings,
Legs yellowed from the heavy cups that
Flattened in a narrow path behind us.
I played with friends along the river.
The thick black mud that sucked
And pulled with subtle temptings, last year
Was mashed and moulded by the stubby fingers
Of my son, aged one.

I came to mountains rubbing softly
Against a low, grey sky, and roads
That curled like worms in on themselves.
I went on border duty
Patrolling an unseen line through a
Sameness of fields and a plethora of
Ditches, drains and little hump-backed bridges.
We bumped along a pot holed road,
Our driver singing as we tried to see
If danger threatened from the skinny hedges
Or squat houses that elbowed one another
In hollows in the hills.

We must have struck a wire.
Before the blast bang shuddered
I floated weightless, disembodied, feet above
The twisted metal pieces that shuddered down
To the flowers and petals of flame
That sprouted below.
The shadows shrank back in the darkness
And drew away from the gaudy advertisement
Of the enemy's presence.
I died in Ireland.

II

I went out with my friends
Boys who had roamed the streets with me
In horse-drawn days, buttermilk sweet,
Haloed by the arcs of skinny legs
Swung wide in swirling skirted circles
Roped round
And round
A lampost.
Our love for life was formed not only in
Dark ringing winter streets of hoarse voiced
play
But days of gold heat coined on sands
And high above, the violin throb of seagulls.
We learned a pride in giant statured heroes
Peopling singing woods
And long robed women trailing love and grief.
No hope to pass with triumph ever young.
No hope.

13

Just passing lives between
The jagged teeth of houses
Straddling the hills. No work. No bond of
feeling
With the hard faced trading men, no singing
In their bones.
And now we wander restless in cold alien
streets
Like a jigsaw half complete
And find ourselves with something real to do.
A cause to fight in peace, to move the world
With moving. Thousands strong we marched.
The clear air surged and sang with us
Until we turned, and soldiers barred the way.
Children -- vicious, sniping, cursing.
Shattered bottles tinkling on the road.
The soldiers moved, shields up, heads down,
Pleating awkwardly with hesitant tortoise
moves.
Some crouched beyond,
Far behind the blue lead barrels.
A child fell slowly, wood smashed head
Trickled curdles of blood,
White hands fluttering an entreaty.
I ran, and tumbled towards him, my stomach
Gaping wide.
And life and love fell from me
As quietly as clouds begauze the pale, flat
Evening sky, star pinned between the
chimneys.
I died for Ireland.

THE OLD PEOPLE

Willie Muldoon lived near us
In a crumbling moulder of stones
With beehives buttoned in the nettles.
He quoted the Bible and hawked great
Pearls of phlegm into the thick lace
Of cow parsley on the road to town.

Sarah Mulligan was tormented by
Some blind, mad ghost of memory
That twitched her eyes.
She feutered as she talked,
Stormy hands pulling at buttons, branches
Or tangled, wanton thoughts.

My granny wore a sack apron
Fastened with a nail, and her eyes
Chipped satisfaction from
A hill field clotted with hay.

They were old.
Blinkered by youth we noticed only
Crabbed hands, sagged ribs, mucoid eyes
And pensioned dreams.

THREE OLD LADIES

Three old ladies murmurous
In dusk dimmed rooms;
A pot pourri of faded hates
And ghosts of love. Their
Voices like gnats' wings
Clouding by the lough
Nip one another. One
Stretches by the window,
Eyes stitching stories
To hang loud and ill fitting
(But neatly finished) on
The passers by.
One fumbles in a corner,
Skirts umbrellaed to the
Thin splayed feet, her
Hands in her lap like
Walnuts wasting. She
Strikes occasionally,
Her venom varnished
With a genteel voice.
The third is restless with
Some book, and dreams of
A rough clad soldier
Slain in family attack.

The air is caught
With crumbling scent.
The clock relentlessly
Negates their feeble
Fumbling attachments.
Shadows draw closer.

DREAM OF AFRICA

I thought of caravans trundled against a
hollow sky
And parrots swaying soundlessly in a poem of
colour,
Even a mellifluent coated lion slutting in
dappled grandeur;
I did not know what flowers would fret the
air,
But the heavy proliferation of purple
bougainvillea,
And the close pale mesh of jacaranda netting
the sun
Thick day, these are of my dreams.

IN THE DRY COUNTRY

We've never been together by the sea.
Your talk of it sweeps cobwebs from my mind.
I see sheep maggoted, cheese holed cliffs,
And feel the skin lash of the flavoured wind.
Trawlers lurching silver drunk and slow.
Sails whipping whitely, crisping flecks of foam.
Steamers munching water; tankers suspended
Dreamlike on the deep distance.
Where is the blood hot, still faced pool,
The restless childhood sea love?
Our children play far, far from the sea,
Baking dryly, like old snake skins shed
On a splintered, thorn-pricked hill.

MAY

Here May is flamboyant,
Big with hibiscus, and dropping oranges
That have plumply suckled on sunshine.
Guavas, thin, pungent and yellow
Burst sweetly in our mouths.
Globes of avocado are pendant
In the cushioned shade of their leaves;
And cups of gold are heavy with blowsy
beauty.
The frangipari is different.
Its flower is delicate, its scent elusive,
And its star shape so deliciously shy
One is shocked at its cold, waxen surface.
But for comfort
There is the rasp of dead dahlias
And the same smart of cut grass
That haunted pearled summer evenings
Strung limpid from mountain to lough.

There the hawthorn ladled its scent
Into hollows in the wind
And one walked silkily on strewn blossom
Scaldies, obscenely raw and gaping
We found cupped comfortably
Among the prickles of the bursting hedge.
And we gathered flowers for the May altar

--- Splashes of bluebells stickily crowning our
fists;
Violets that peered from the hedge bottom
Like uncertain children;
Anemones that spangled the wood;
And bursts of celandine that gleamed
Above their dark leaves like women in furs.
They were stuck in meat paste jars
Around the statue of Our Lady
Brought from Knock. ·
At dusk it rises like a ghost
Above the crushed Spring smell.

JACK 1974

The hot days enervated him.
It did not show, when, like Icharus
Courage taut as membrane
Over cross nailed wood, he
Launched, nose held tight, into
An alien element.
He would crouch for long minutes
Watching a cricket pulse into
Tense light flight.
Or, Cuthbert camel by his side,
Snake hunt in the long, sharp stalks
Of black jacked grass.

But in the thin light of the candle
Story comforted and slack in bed,
Witches blackened and blighted
The shadows by the door.
The blue rim of his lips gleamed and
quavered.

At home, where long forgotten winds came
Bone rattling, skirling, and plaiting the dark,
He grew.

NOVEMBER IN SWAZILAND

You walked upon the jacaranda blossom
Lightly. The bells lay soundless on the grass.
Dumb wide mouths and scent of moonless
nights
And whispering leaf blades crouching as you
passed.

I waited in the soft mouthed candle light,
Moth wings flicking sharp against the pane
Splinters of sound that fretted, fluttering
heartbeats
Shuddering back into the heavy night,
Falling like broken moonbeams
Shattered on the jacaranda tree.

Fingers whispering their message
Muted music
Singing of joy, of plangent sorrow;
Dark places
Where the night tainted feathers
And furrows hide pain.
Scarlet dancing dreams spinning slowly down
to lie
Defenceless in the hollow of your hand.

FOR P.M.

Do you start in your sleep at the frail, curled touch
Of its hand?
Your son who would have paced
Your land with you,
Measuring a future in every grass clogged step.
A small stick of a boy
Who ached for hobnails like his granda
And had thin, white, ticklish ankles
Just like you.
Perhaps it was your daughter, brown and dainty,
Who wove in daisy chains the pride of love possessing
And harnessed you.
Dream to never waken;
To feel the light, damp clasp, to see
The blurred blue loveliness of ignorant eyes.
How can it be? One set of wrinkles is
Like another. Bent limbs.
A bi-furcated animal,
But yours, you.
Ah God, it's gone.

AFRICAN NIGHT

A moth got squashed between your pages
As your eyes split stony would have murdered
me.
It died as surely as its brothers,
Spluttering damp minute breakers of the
candle blur.
Whiskey soured we stared, cut open wounds,
And cauterised and sewed with faulty thread.
I nibbled at the respite
Urgent as an ant swarm dragging at an outsize
crumb
Until you turned
Wearily
And in the cacophonous frog hoarse night
We crumpled, both defeated.

YOU LEFT THE MUSIC

You left the music there unfinished.

I found it, on someone else's table,
The notes scratched. I wished
You'd not made promises to nibble
At when hollow hunger ambushed.

MOWILLIAN

Somewhere along the line
The loanin turned into a lane
And the jamb wall disappeared.
A new villa rose on the old
Thorn's mangled site, bold
On the hillside, wonderfully pared.

The boor trees' blooms are frittered.
The corncrake no longer patterns
The sweep of long, sweet summers.
And yet, yet still the small moss
Cheeper haunts the walled
Slopes, a brave, unfettered cantor.

The forth, too, stands; a nest of trees
Cradling the seasons' certainties.

IRELAND

How many times have schoolboys
Bent to draw a map of Ireland?
Tautened tongue tips guiding
Wavering lines of green and
Scarlet wombs of cities. Their
Eyes aren't straight. They
Slide from strategy to secrets.
Men have fought for these. Pale
Husks veined with attitudes
And gaudy dreams. When
The last line is ruled, no bugle blows.
They bend to push their pens again.

TEN YEARS ON

We live together somehow.
We get along well they say
And I smile with them. Now
And again the grey
Of the city is dusted
With sunshine, mustiness
Routed in a scuttling wind.
We pare the thick rind
From our thoughts to get
To the core. Sometimes my
Teeth stick in the flesh.
You choke, don't bother to try.
I live in my words
But you hoard yours ---
An old wine that drips
Like vinegar, shrivels my lips.

YOU'VE GONE FISHING

You've gone fishing
And the room is empty.
Soul songs have sung
Themselves asleep. I
Sink in the night, leafless
At last, while silence
Breathes in the children's room.

ON REFLECTION

And night, that shrinks around
The keen, wild whistle of a train
Becomes reflection. Sudden
Bloodbeats work against the grain

And you, alarmed at this,
At the heated, devilled dreaming,
Hesitate. One step beyond
Puts every dear long feeling

In jeopardy. One only.
Poise. Balance. You can't cease swaying,
Going and coming. Love will
Settle to net you safely.

So, not seeing, not blindly,
Open-eyed you face away.

WALKING DOWN SOME ROADS
IS PAINFUL

Walking down some roads is painful.
Bone shreds thread cracks
In the pavement like a Chinese
Lantern flickering under trees.
Apart from trodden ways
Couched heather shackled
The clean knob of your ankle.
Once, between the gatehouses,
Beyond us, beyond the
Whipping wind, a dual
Skulled lightning shaft split
Our very hands apart. By
The river you showed white
Bellied fish slabbed on
Thick water. I'd to fight
Brambles, but kept my balance.

EVENING ON THE RIVER

Sprawled on the river bank rabbit rich
Eyes moving with the water's withering
Waste, the slow contented leech
Of thoughts bloats itself on evening.
March Brown, Coch-y-Bondhu, -- ease and
Flick, tease the flint worn turn.
Tease burrs from hopes lambed
Coldly, fattened in haste, worn
Thin with worms of rancour. Catch
A quickening gleam. A spotted gem,
Slick smooth sides and eyes hatching
Dullness. Drowning garden
Of pleasant melancholy.

A CRYSTAL BIRD

I want a crystal bird in a
Cage of fern.
I want some honeyed kisses.
A brown stone urn.
Give me last year's wine, a
Broken lute.
Give me words of love in an
Unfinished book.
I've got secrets. I've got limbs
Of fire and bone.
I've got your reflection in my eyes.
I'm alone.
I want some crystal kisses,
A brown stone fern.

ALL I ASK

All I ask is to find myself.
Face gone in the mouth of the mirror
My voice soars soundless.
My hands rifled your treasures.
Feet echoed yours. Slack on the shelf
Of my stomach you rested.
Rain pats the roof with remembering fingers.

LIMBO

I keep waiting for the grand gesture,
Something that will rivet stars thrown
Carelessly into my darkness. They
Will crack as they cool, the splinters
Shaggy spearheads of our newness.
You will ripple and I'll rebound
Startled, the clouds straining apart.

I THOUGHT YOU WERE FOLLOWING

'I thought you were following,' he said
And turned on the green. His gaze
Was towards the sea slipping past
To Derry, and towards the boats fast
In the harbour. Mine bent to the
Crushed scent of his passing, to note
Only a broken stem and one small
Shell that housed the water's secret call.

TRAVELLING HOME

Travelling in our small world, back from
Derry, light sliced a secret summer room.
Hair, a hand moving upward. We passed
On unobserved and spoke in lower tones.
On the back seat the three sat apart.
Only their eyes betrayed them, sealed
Momentarily and coming back to life
As we slipped on. Darkening fields
Were suddenly hostile shapes that made
Our breathing settle heavy, sucking night
In on ourselves, and every move
Seemed boneless. All that was outside
Leaned on the glass. You steered precisely,
Steadily. And then thumb slack,
At the journey's end, the little one
Sang, leaning on your back.

UP SLIEVE GALLION

Curlew calls tautened the sky; my skin
Crawled in that crystallised keening
As we stumbled on the stony path.
Slieve Gallion on a Sunday evening.
The views were disparate, tugging
Us right and left. Below -- the lough
The plain, settlements hugging
Fattened fields and snuggling trees.
Beyond -- blue hills, lap after lap,
Suggesting, concealing, trout stream,
Solitude, soul's measuring.
Two grey crows fought between
Crags. The resident wind freely
Buffeted us this way and that.
But there was no choice really.
The last low rays smoothed the road home.

DADDIES' GIRLS

'Who's Daddy's girl? She looks
Just like her Mammy.' Good.
He'll notice me and I'll
Be the beloved child.
'She's got a boyfriend. Yes.
You know his family, at least
His mother. I'm pleased.'
His touch, his smile release
A catch. I'm normal.
I've done the right thing for a
Change. 'What a lovely
House! So big! Above
The usual run. He must
Make a regular fuss
Of you.' Oh yes, I know.
He's nine to five, no
Working late. I've all
Mod cons. Small
Wonder that my smile
Is pasted permanently.
'Isn't she sweet! Just
Like her Mammy. The first
Gets so much attention

Don't forget to mention
That you love him too.'
Fingers clutch me smoothly.
The circle tightens. Together
We can break out. Daddies' girls.

CATHY IS DEAD

Cathy is dead.
In each of us lies a small winter.
Rawness branches against the pallor of her peace.
Winds startle us. Eyes to the window, looking.
We huddle for warmth. Arms offer ease.
Murmurs catch breath. Limbs move to comfort.
Stillness evades us, we wander from room to room.
Petals fall, the green grain of snowdrop exposed.
There's frost in that moon.
And Cathy is dead.

WRECKED

When their craft became unsure
They foundered, beached here
On shifting ground. What
Depths were sounded, memories
Cast up to plaster widening
Crevices? And yet she held
The ring that could have saved
Them both intact. It caught
On the moon bones, shattering
Into bits that slipped wide
Through all the grasping fingers,
Washed far out on the morning tide.

MAN SHOT IN COUNTY TYRONE

Afterwards
No birds sang for a full month.

The neighbours were agreed, he'd
Only gone into the hayfield
While the others, caps on knees,

Settled loosely on their hard backed
Chairs to savour a while's crack
And scrub their fills of tobacco.

He'd gone because the hay was his.
He needed to be silent in the
Loosening swathes that ribbed

The breathing hillside. He needed
Too, to touch it, fondling seed heads,
Biting stalks, bending over at

The low end to burrow a question
In the heavy still damp freshness.
That was when they shot him,

The soldiers who had squatted
In the dark, and in the morning, that
An arms cache might be spotted.

No arms were found, they've said,
Not on, nor near, the broken hay-
Caught body, lapped in silence.

JUST SUPPOSE

Suppose, just suppose, when you
Turned the corner, away from me,
My life really stopped. Caught,
Mouth framing your name, they'd see.......
What? A block of salt crumbling quietly
Shivering loose some grains to
Spit on the floor. Or, backed up,
At one with the lintel, stony
Breathed, hardened in lapsed
Many childed shape. Old Sheelagh
Na Gig, cold and still open.
Stalled, willing to yield.
Your feet could crumple me. I'd
Have no eyelids to stop the sight.

THUS FAR AND NO FURTHER

To leave the house is difficult, to put
The cool, comfortable key
Above the door, latch the gate, set foot
On the stone bound way.
There's crack in the village we pass, taking
Pains to the ruffled shore,
Greeting the trippers we meet. Wait.
At the end of the day we're alone.
Shrill on our ears the starlight breaks.
Whole dominions wrestle in a sigh.
Come thus far we halt, proud waves
Broken. Nervously
We turn to each other, confusing despair
And wonder, pounding at the heart's closed door.

A WET BANK HOLIDAY IN PORTRUSH

Main Street morning-empty.
Windows held cloud, china, hooks,
Hamburgers fashioned from rock.
The car park slept. Two small
Surfers huddled in a shelter,
Their boards casual on the beach.

By noon, hooded figures
Sprachled into the wind.
Feet sped by, gutties, espadrilles,
Sandals with winking toes-
Doubled in puddles, slapping the
Pavement, scobing the sand.

Evening opened. A family picknicked
On a purple rug. Raindrops tickled
The writhing sea, while ferris girls,
Clamouring gulls, clutched
Pebble voiced boys who
Weren't
Afraid.

MID-LIFE CRISIS

Like salmon questioning the falls
We strove. We've coasted calms,
Beached in Indian wealth of Autumn.
Smoke has tangled in the fire

Of my hair, clouding my eyes.
I heave the bundled shelter off
My dreams, bivouac by yours.
Some night, safe in shelter, free of

Wolf, of water, blades of cold, one of
Us will strike; the one remaining will
Readjust, clamp the chanting mouth;
Close the gap; stay, perfectly still.

What if breathing itself becomes treacherous?
We'll trust, trust each the other's helplessness.

COFFEE AND LAVENDER

My rooms all lean together;
Interlock; mingle lemons, garlic,
Coffee and lavender; places where
People come to slumber, to frolic.

The people who come to these rooms
Laugh a great deal;
Eat prodigiously of pieces broken,
Argue for real.

I scurry, plan, smile and
Wonder who really belongs here;
Wonder what will stifle the
Rank goat smell, wild bee of my honey.

I wonder too, why I slide
Open my doors so welcome wide.

INTERLUDE

All over the city
In the mouth of evening
Women are waiting.
In steaming kitchens
In cooling bedrooms
In flickering lounges
Women are waiting.
And in a hotel
One woman waits,
With a cracked glass,
a silken glove
And a twisting smile.

IF NO-ONE COMES
(for Annie)

If no-one comes
Will the dust motes breed?
What plants push fronds
Frenziedly over them to feed
On my air? I find this
Burden of light, forcing
The corners apart, persists
In spite, overpowering
All I do to salve my eyes
Assaulted by emptiness.

If no-one comes
Will the shadows meet?
What small winged irritant
Harrows the afternoon, pleating
Little sounds around the blind?
The crack in the china bleeds
Across, exploding spiderlines
To fuse wingbeat and heartbeat,
Both measuring. My blurred
Core crouches off centre.

If no-one comes
Will the dark lie down?
What worm slips against
The wood, searching round

For one crevice, just the
Right size for a wormish
Shape? I cannot see
In this. My hands push
Away. All I come up against
Are my own bones peeling.

WINTER WALK

Note the branches of that elm
Spread like fingers to the fire;
The plated water offering
Back a pallid host. Air
Smartly rings us, carefully
Stepping in tune, while the
Wind's knife wickedly pares
Our features. Thorns sieve
Fieldfares to leaven the
Afternoon, and we discuss
Love, pain, children, the months
That eloquently pass us
By. We turn then, back into our
Lengthening shadows, and our feet
Respond clumsily to the call to
Hasten home to the sweetness
Of burning ash, wholesome bread,
Wine to savour, our table set.
A journey's end when all is said;
Keep moving then. We'll weather it.

NOSTALGIA

The pungent spices I grind for your vindaloo
Awake no echoes here. The snip of scallions into
Champ was more in her line. And
The nutmeg
Rolling in a drawer was antidote
To something
Or other, not used to glaze the rice.
A wheen
Of sultanas glorified her soda scones.
Christmas Eve
Brought oranges aching with fragrant
Foreignness.
Travelling far, lured on by vagrant
Essences
I found the kernel, a cracked stone
That ringed
The images I thought I'd flown.

TIMOR MORTIS

1

He lies patient in the
Sterile room, and I
Foreshortened by this meek
Withdrawal, bend my
Shoulder, take on the pack,
And face, with little grace,
The rigours of the road.

There's no turning back. He
Who paved the way with giant
Strides, has deserted. The
Corner is his world. Faint
I hear the feet behind my back.
Into one head crams everything. Braced,
Helpless, I accept the load.

2

Cries in the night, like linen shredding,
Rip jagged, fret the stretched ear
Till the coil of darkness, shrinking
Blots like flannel on the tongue. All hear
Them calling, some from far grass blown
Where the corncrake still saws at the dark.
Others are nearer, come combing with wolf bone
The skin that slips over us, roughened like bark.

3

Stranger in the icy bed
I tolerate you. Sliding
Silently in, touching
Your toes to mine. I
Feel your entry an affront.
If I don't look, don't greet
You, hold my arms crossed
Over my breasts, surely
You must leave, unsatisfied.

GROWING PAINS

She got her hair bobbed
Sleek to the nape.
A sudden adult narrowness
Sidled into her eye
As she fronted the mirror.
Her back lengthened
And a new gentleness tucked
Itself beside her mouth.

'What happened your hair?' he asked,
Dismayed as I was when
Her whole face crumpled.

MAKING MUSIC

An old trumpeter blows softly
Now, his breath misting the
Notes that circle close.
His fingers push and ease,
Slide with warm familiarity.
His used lips rasp against
The instrument, scabbing old tunes.
She sags below him, waving
Away the coloured charms,
And minds him vibrant --
Weaving pretty traps for pretty girls,
Fresh songs in dewy others.
The last throb fades.
The cracking smile pulls
From her a lullaby,
A keen, a low lament.

FAMILY OUTING

Another Sunday, and in Autumn,
We returned to Doagh. This time
The stone rocked under us and
The rip of the tide distracted all
Our eyes from the further shore.
'There's not an air,' someone said.
Boomfall of feet on sandy hills.
Cropped grass scratching like notes
Not quite true. And so we climbed,
And photographed, and talked. A
Family outing. Three generations
Fitting together roundly, building
A store of sharing where the treasure
In the dark and the ladder prudently
Raised keep our tower inviolate.

OPENED EYES
(or the Song of Eve)

Keep touching me. I need your closeness,
Your breath, your whispers. Fill the gap
As fireweed does, surprising with loveliness
Bomb scarred streets. This is today,
Is yesterday. Same skin on both, soft as
Wings on dusty butterflies, flitting from my
Nose to yours, my lips to yours, here, on this grass,
Their wing breaths no stronger than the sighs
We made. They've left us now. And this
Is hard to understand -- how one moment
Moves to the next, as water slips
Over stone and sand, no evidence
Of movement, of change, until it's broken
Into shivers, by wind or fish or foot.
What split our moments into then
And now? What changed us, the root
Of us, from shy soft stroking cuddles
Eye to eye, to this slick panting race --
Your toes scrabbling in earth and mud,
My vision fastened on stars and space?

I DESERVE A REST

Sunday afternoon. I can relax.
I've finished, all redd up for now.
I'm quite pleased with the result
Of all that work. It's not been easy.
Decisions! Decisions! But really it's
All a matter of organization. Planning.
Lists. What can I tick off?

Light -- it's in place, tenting under
The sheet of space.
Darkness -- waiting in the wings,
Tired wrestling,
For light has pinpointed its
Tiny weaknesses
And stars keep breaking through.

Sun and moon -- ripe for work;
Shifts, of course.
Water -- it was fun doing water;
The laughter
Of rivers, the scolding of falls,
Mild loughs,
Oceans that fret, bluster, brood.

I sloshed on colour to give
It a lift.
But it lacked something extra --
Zip, pizazz.
I added more movement, high waves and
Strong winds.
I realised then what else I should do.

I created life, in various forms --
Scaly, furry,
Smooth; growing rooted and free.
Swim! Leap!
Crawl! Slither! Walk! Climb!
Run! Fly!
The sheer thrill of the new!

I'm tired today. I started it off.
But I can't be expected to keep
Watching over it all, all of
The time. So here's the best bit!
I've let some of them THINK
And reason and create within
Limits, of course. So now -- forty winks.
Oh me! I forgot about sin.

There's always tomorrow.

NEAR BENONE

Flung like scraps of burnt paper
Your words drifted above my head.
An autumn evening brought us together
Shoulder to shoulder. Birds fed
In the shallow estuary. Brent
Geese clucked contented. Curlews
Mourning creased my skin. You
Wanted more, more than I or
The evening could yield. So, apart
From everything, frozen to the core,
We shuffled leadenly towards accord.

FOR GRANNY J.

Early November, in the dark of the moon,
Whenever winds come stealing from the west, then
The eels go back into the Sargasso Sea.
That is what they say, the fishermen at Toome.
Late October we felt that wind swaddle the
Room where you lay happed, blind with intensity
A clamour in your blood to go. You slipped from
Our clutches, vexing our grasp, betraying
Us once and for all. This moon-pull was urgent;
You cut through the roots. A frisson of freedom,
A flick -- you were gone in spite of our praying,
Setting us adrift without star, chart, sextant.
Lost ones, lonely ones, keen for reality,
Our only comfort lies in the seamless sea.

THE COMET IS COMING

The comet is coming
And I, wondering if
This means death, birth
Or a new adventure
Go to gaze.

It's hard to see among
The roofs. each one
Harbouring dreams and
Hopes. But there it is,
Unruly blaze

That makes us feel like
Grains of rice, mites,
Specks too small to
Mean much beyond
Ourselves. I don't

Like this. My neck aches.
I cannot take cold beauty.
Lamp light drizzles over
Stones, easing me. My feet
Stumble, at home.

AT REST

I have come this far
And sit untrammelled
In a city garden
Rimmed with a hum of distance.

Here bees are busy
And ants, with small
Determinations soldier on.
Hands are hollow,
Feet fiercely still.

Behind -- a girl,
Bold as a scarlet tulip
Slender and young.